Trucks, Planes and Cars Coloring Book For Kids

This book belongs to:

DUMP TRUCK

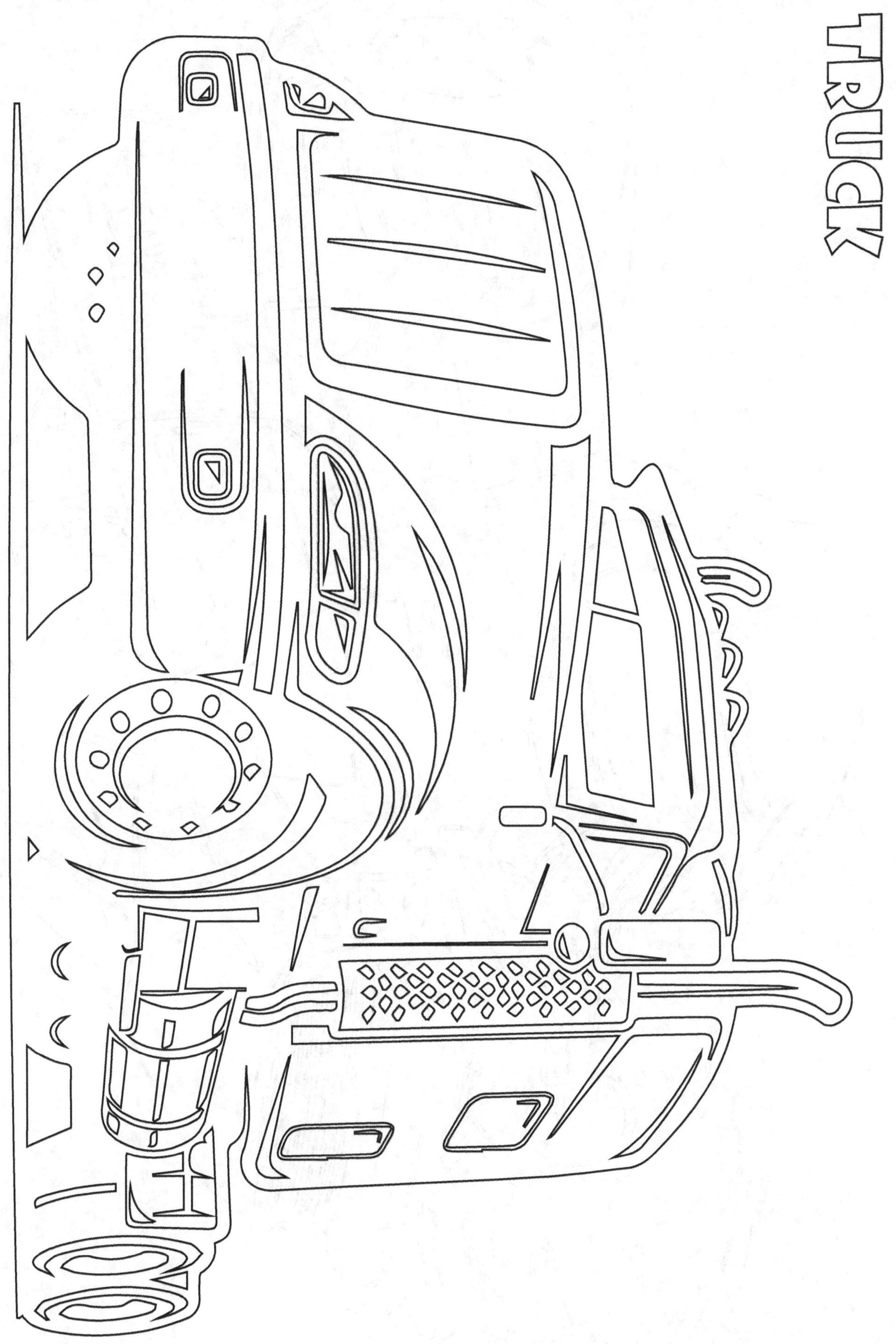

TRUCK

MONSTER TRUCK

TIPPER TRUCK

GARBAGE TRUCK

FUEL TRUCK

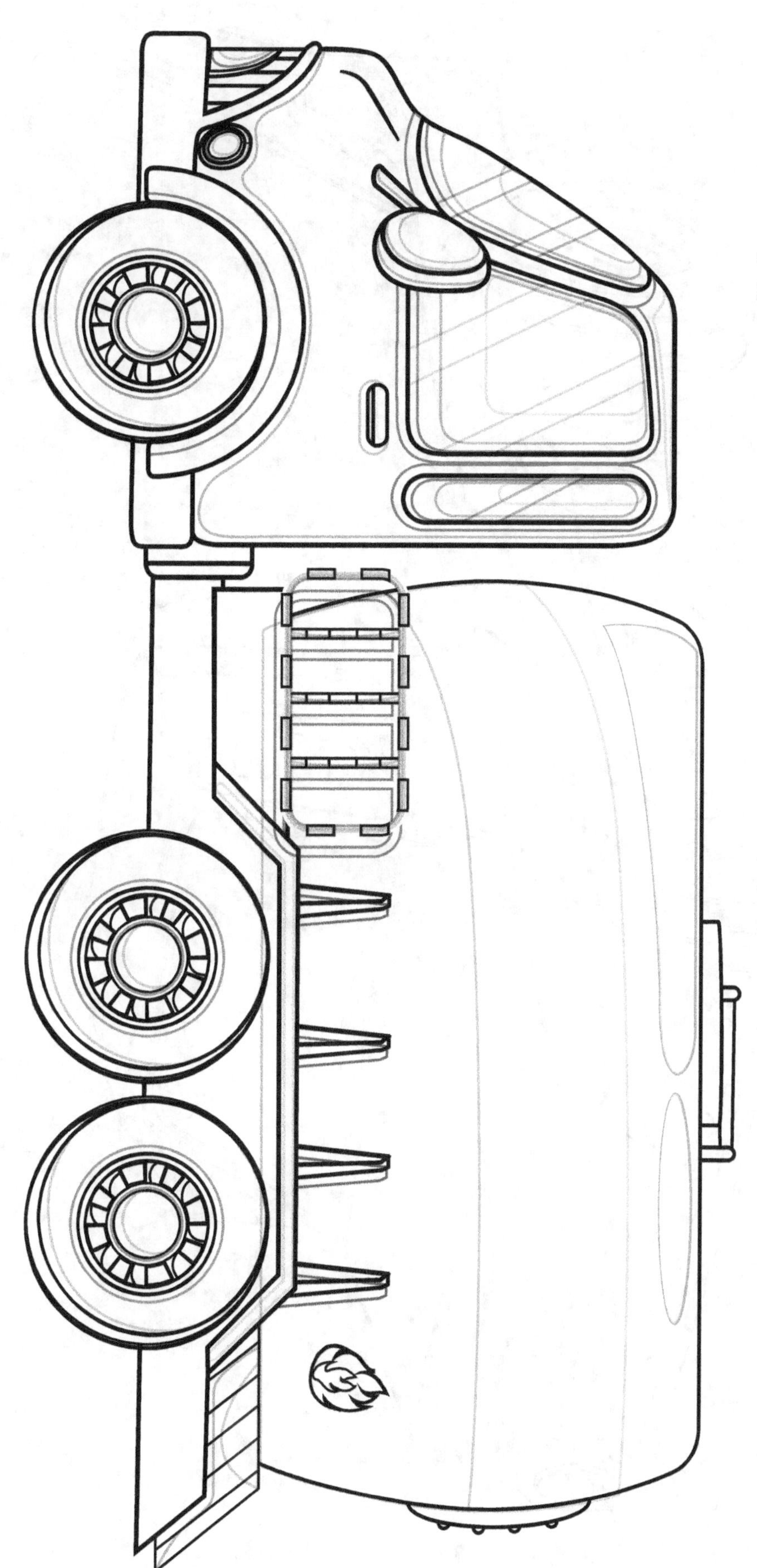

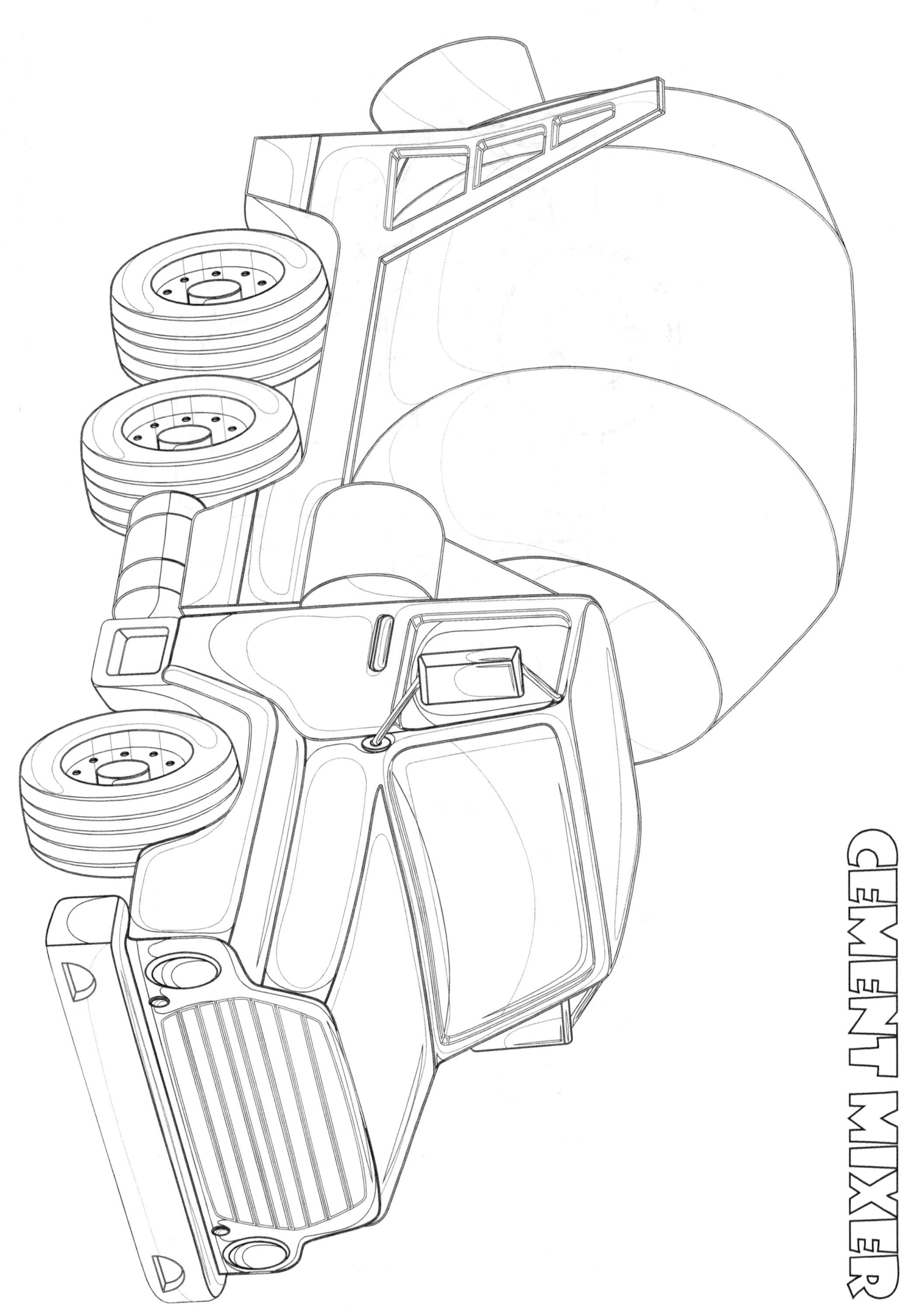
CEMENT MIXER

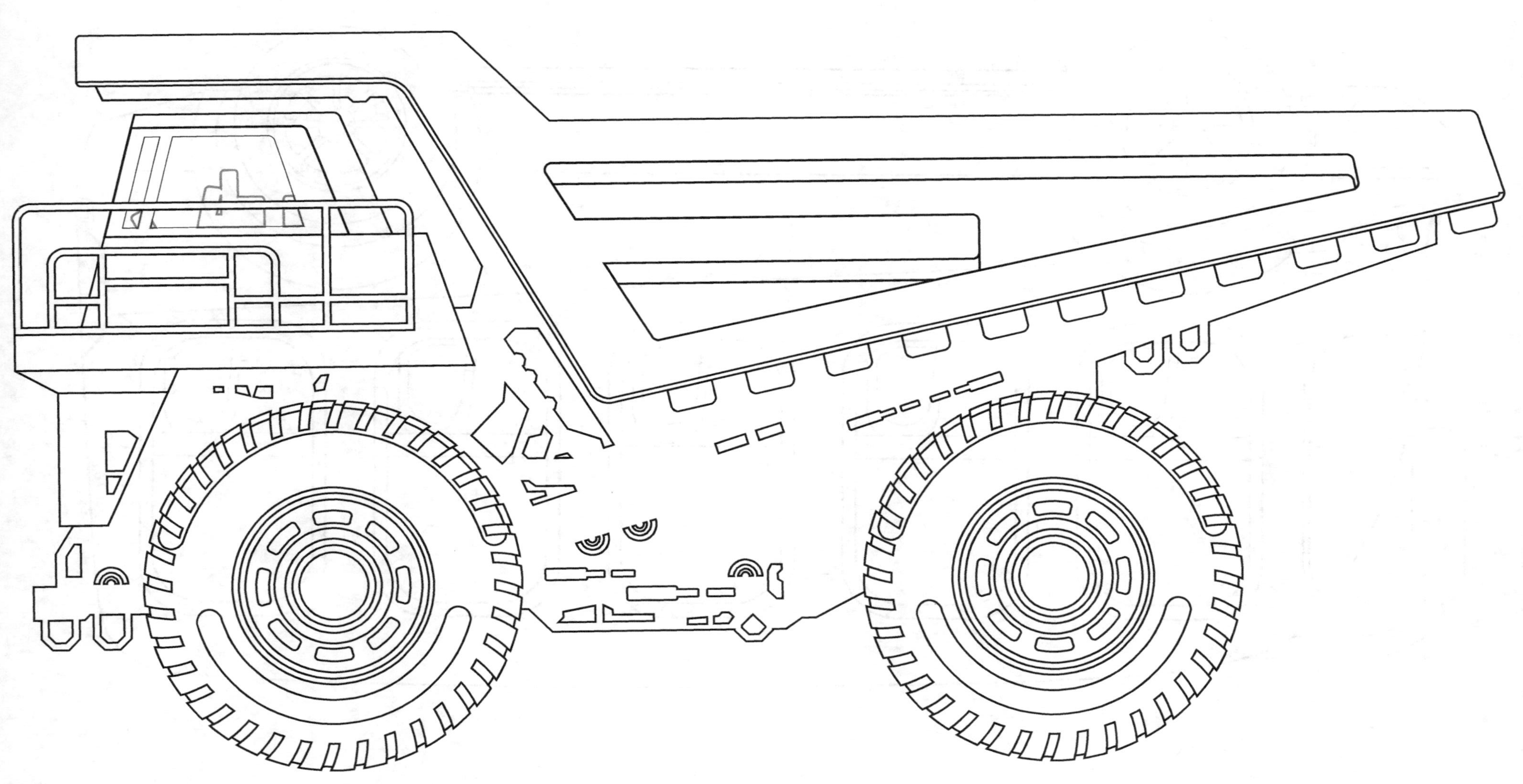

MINING DUMP TRUCK

MINI BUS

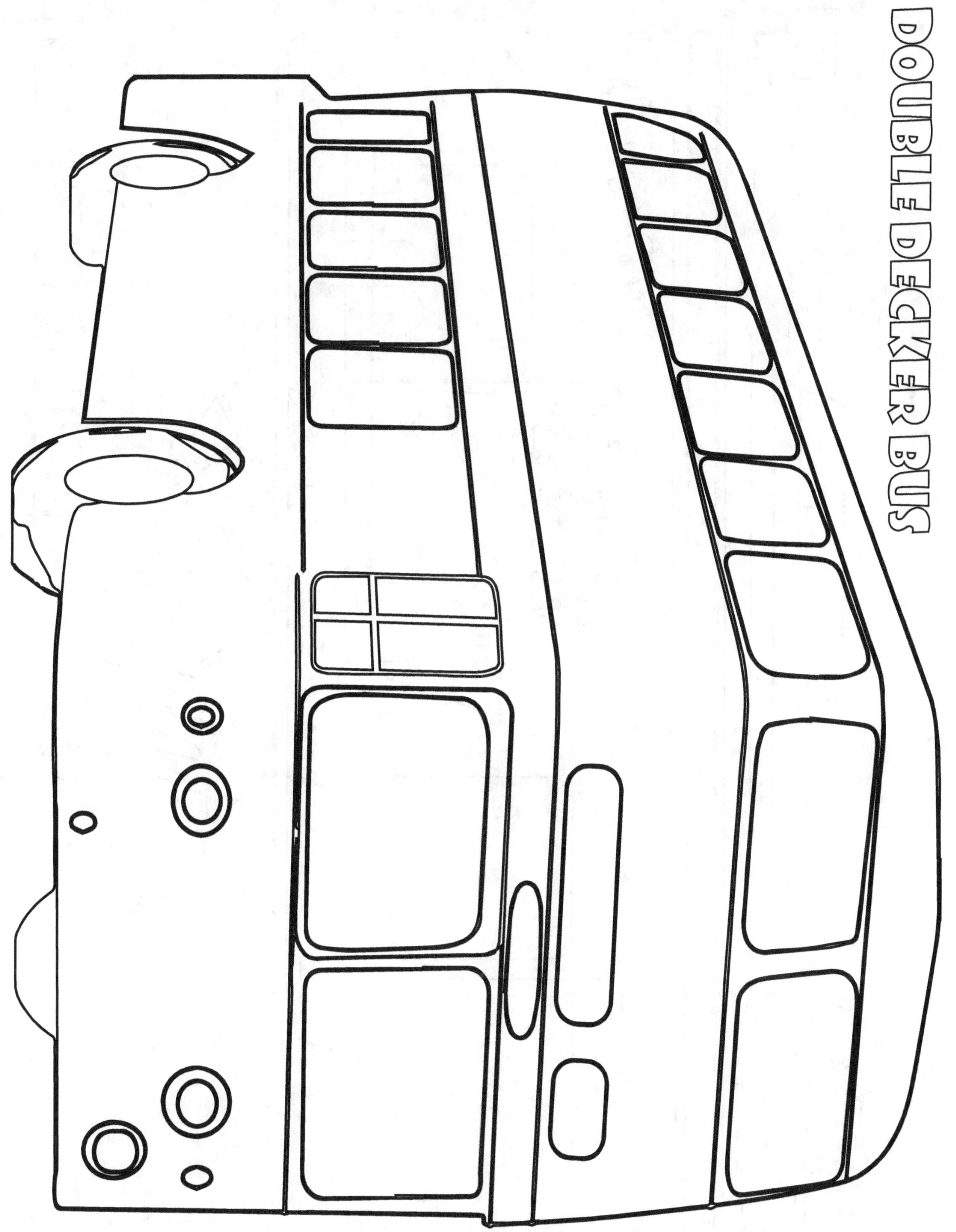

DOUBLE DECKER BUS

ICE CREAM TRUCK

TRACTOR TRAILER

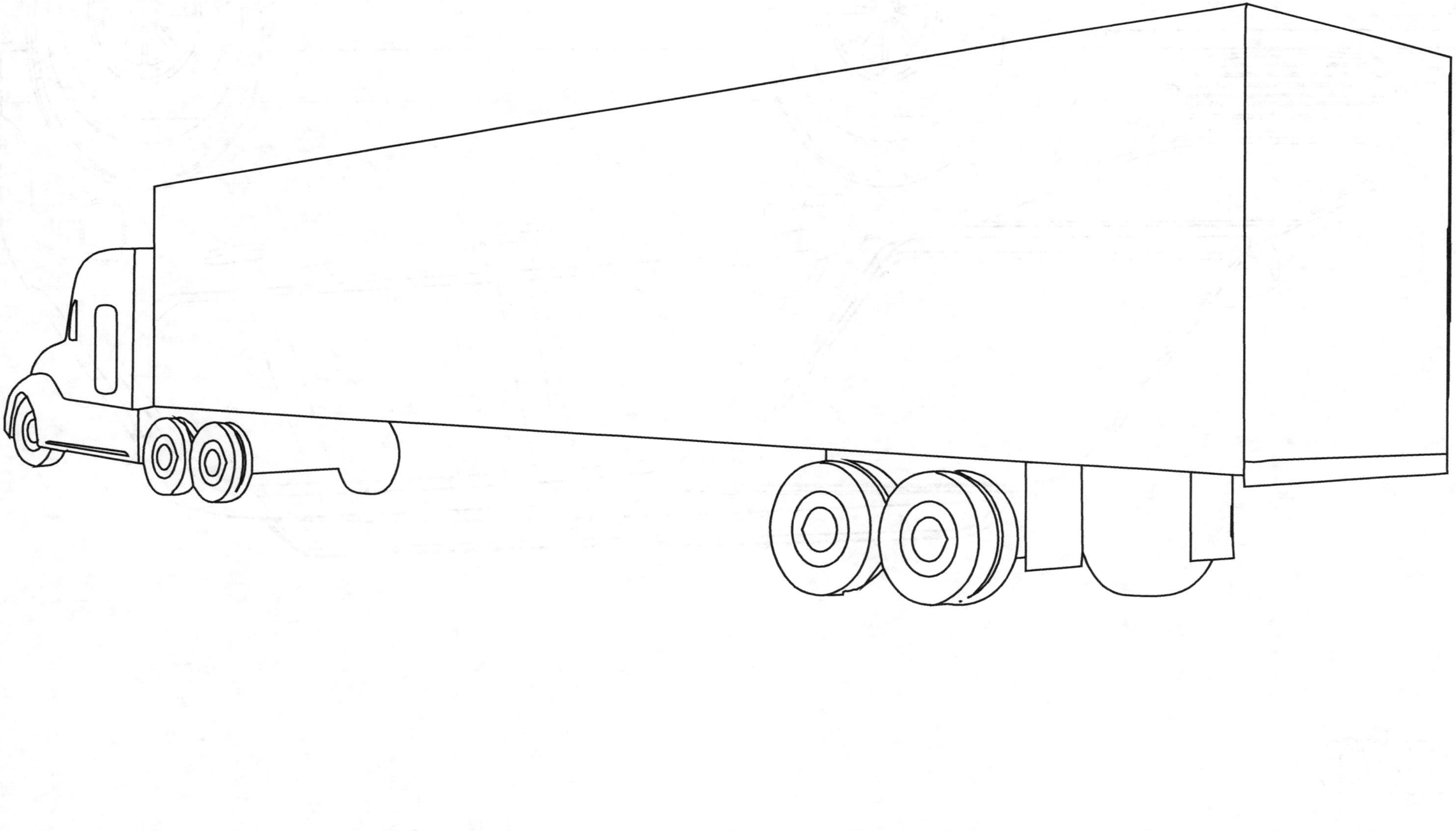

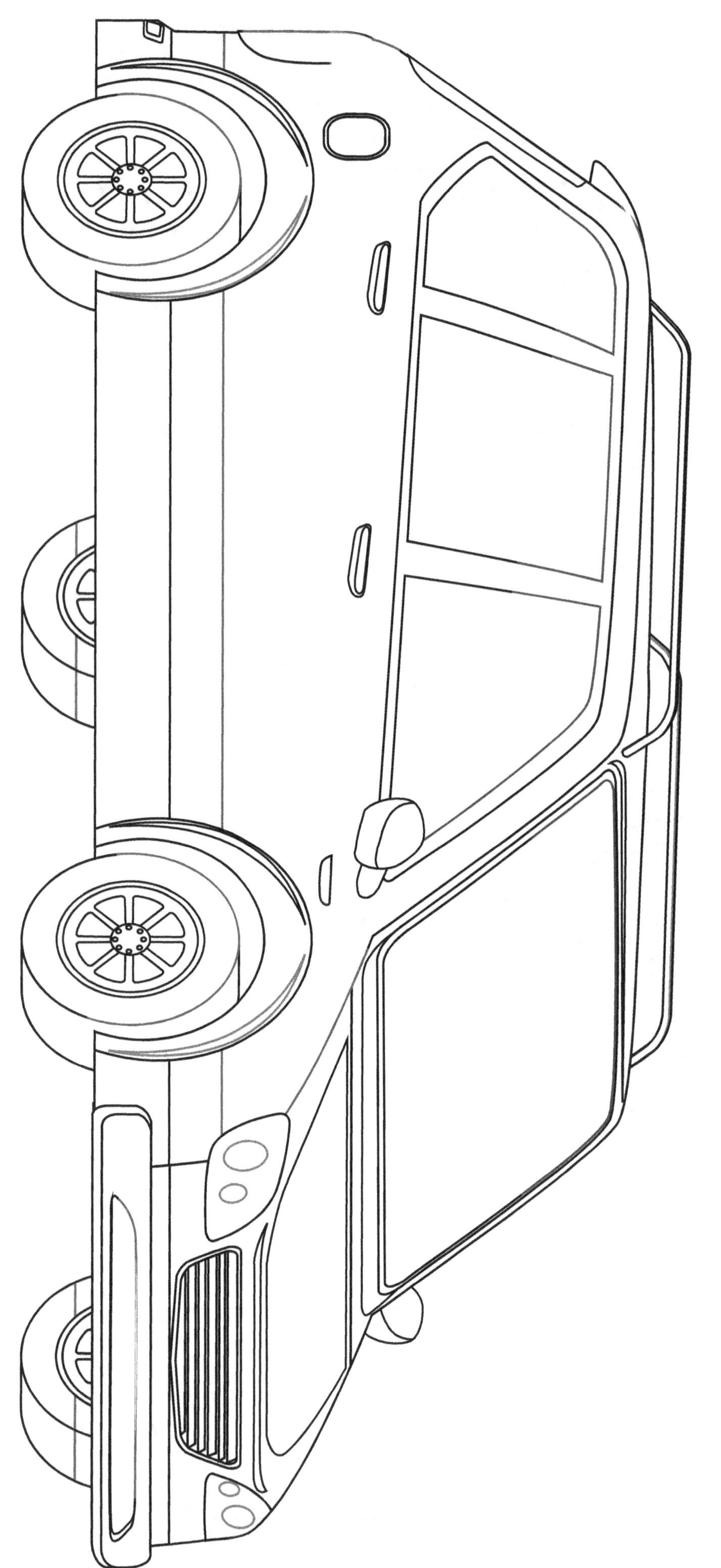

CAR

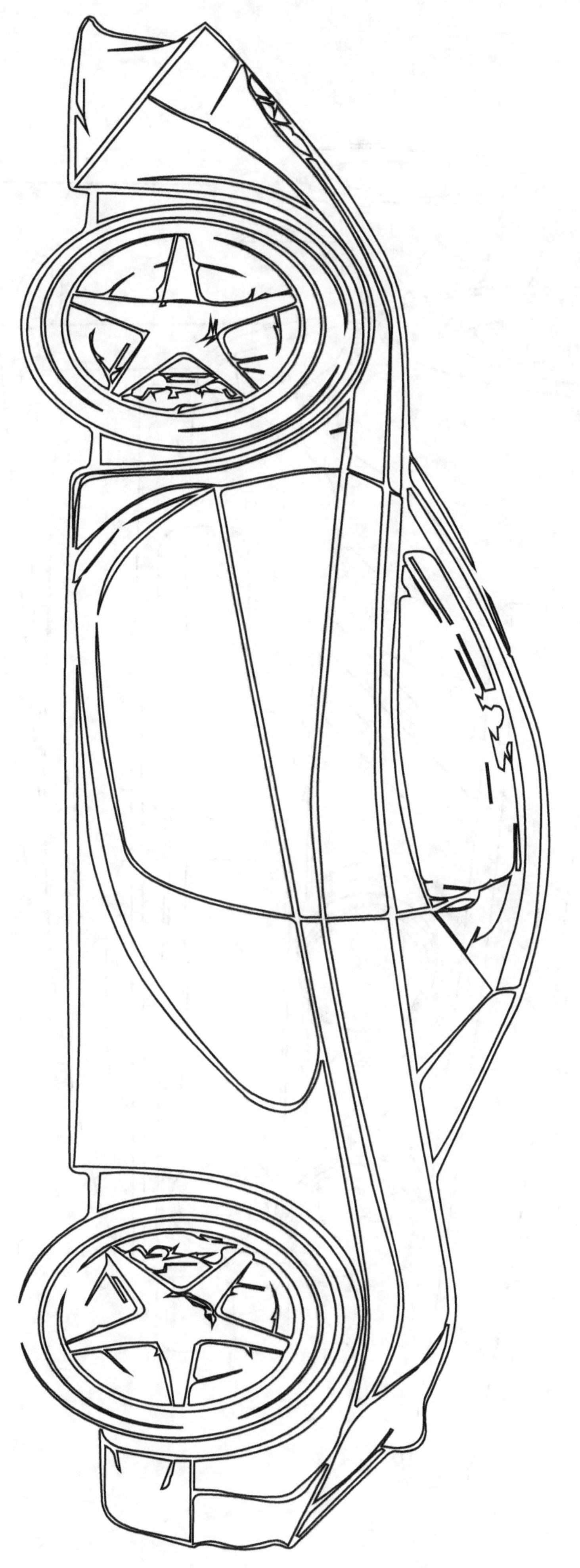

SPORT CAR

JEEP

FAMILY CAR

AMBULANCE

POLICE CAR

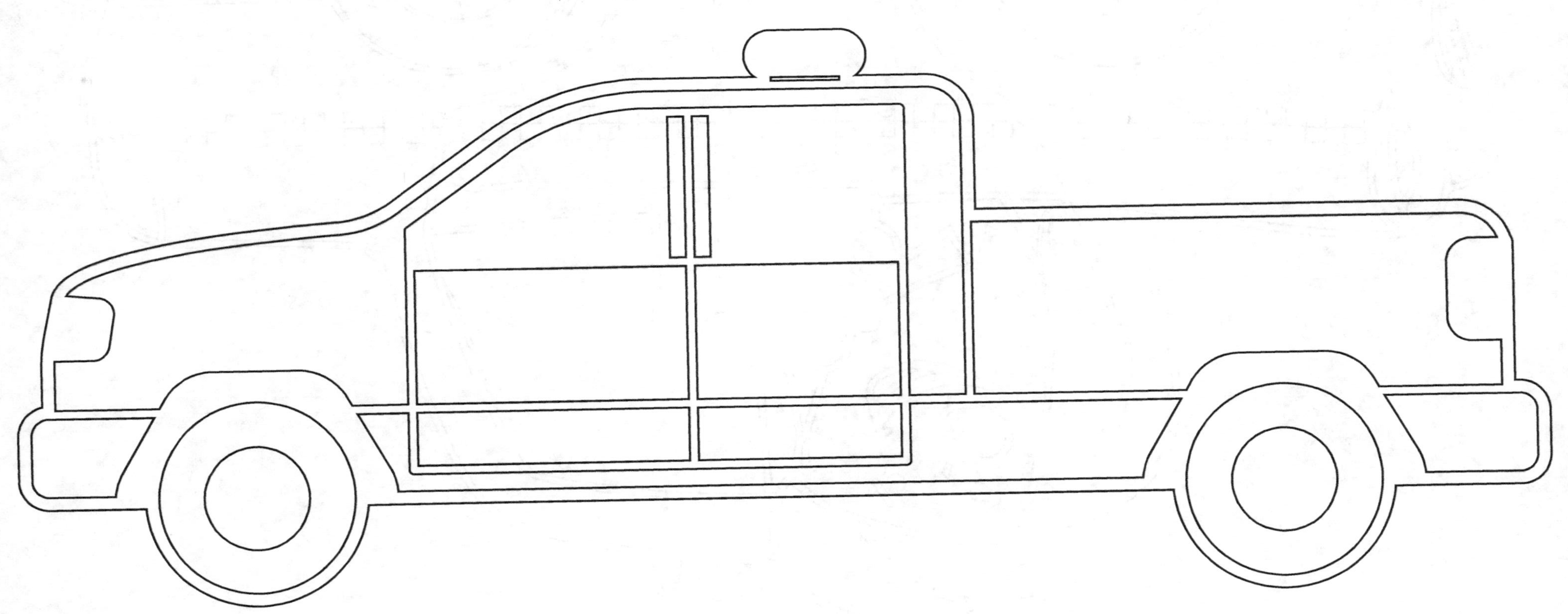

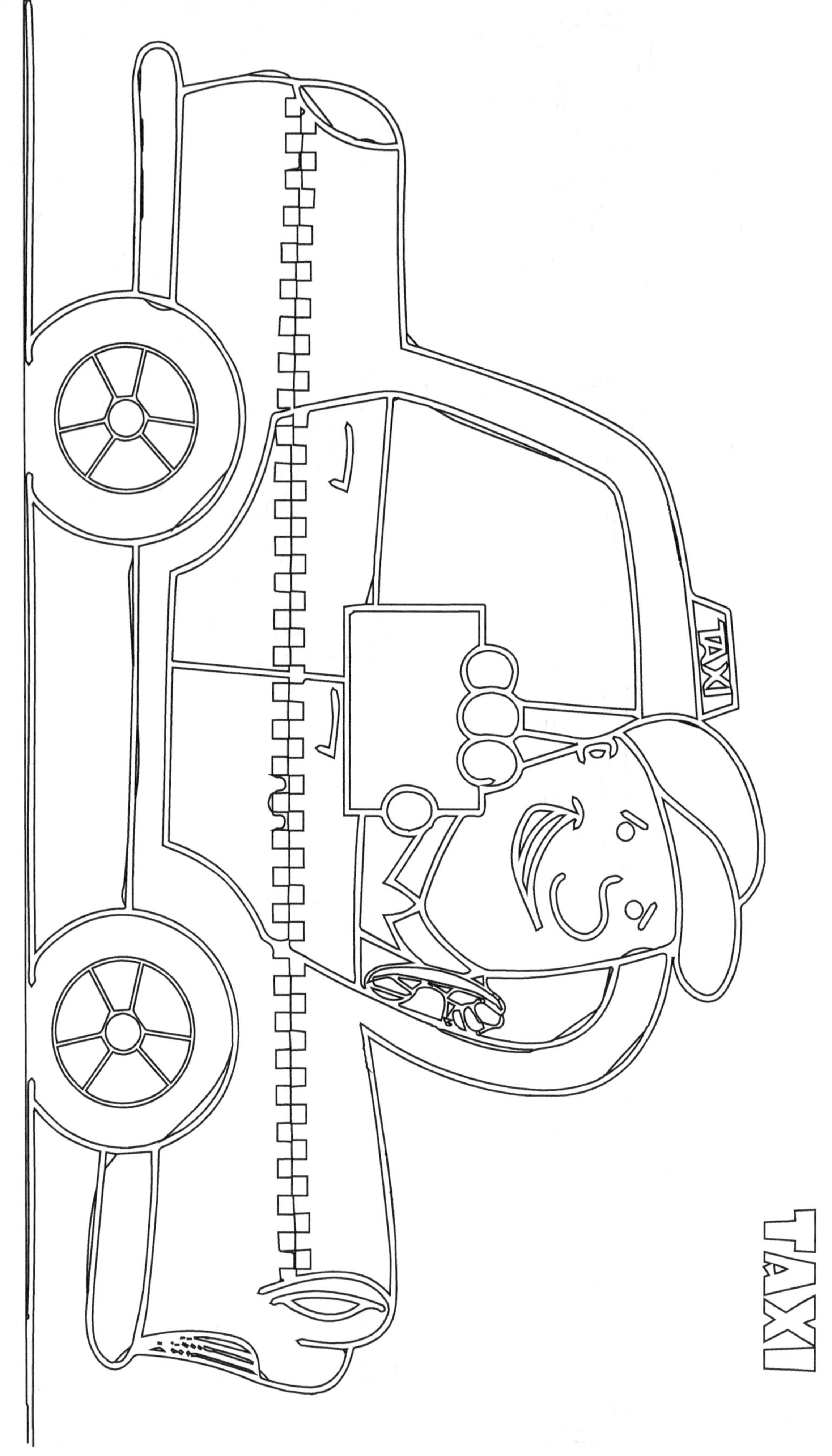

TAXI
TAXI

TOW CAR

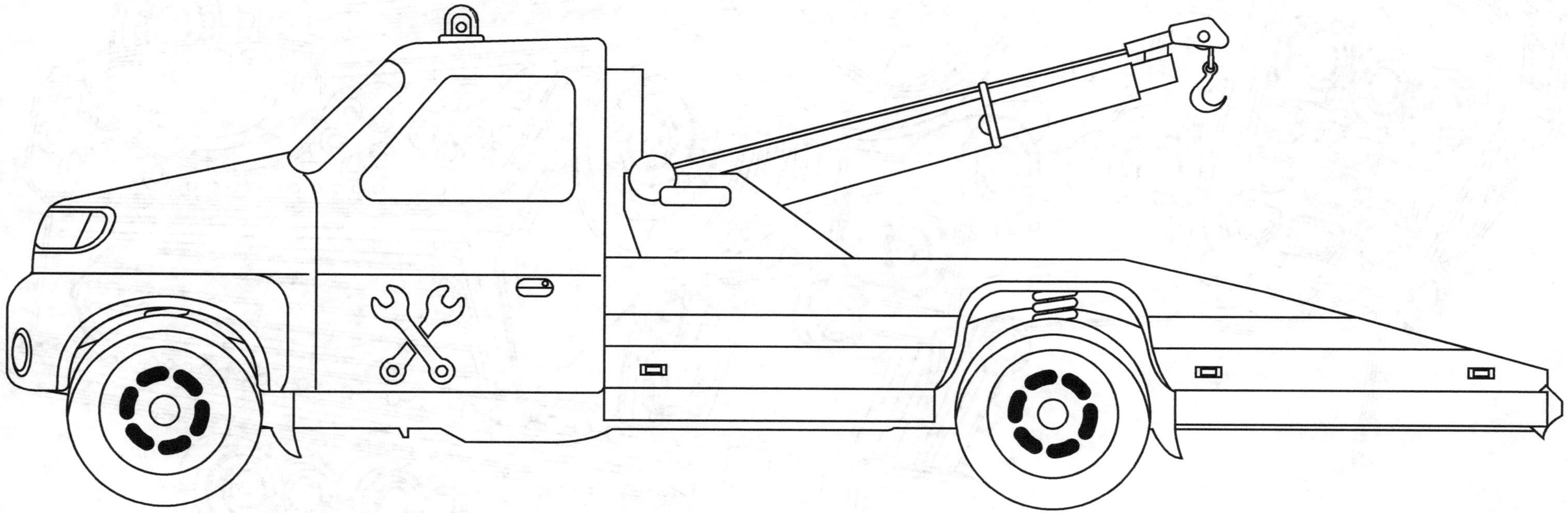

JEEPNEY CAR

PERSONAL CAR

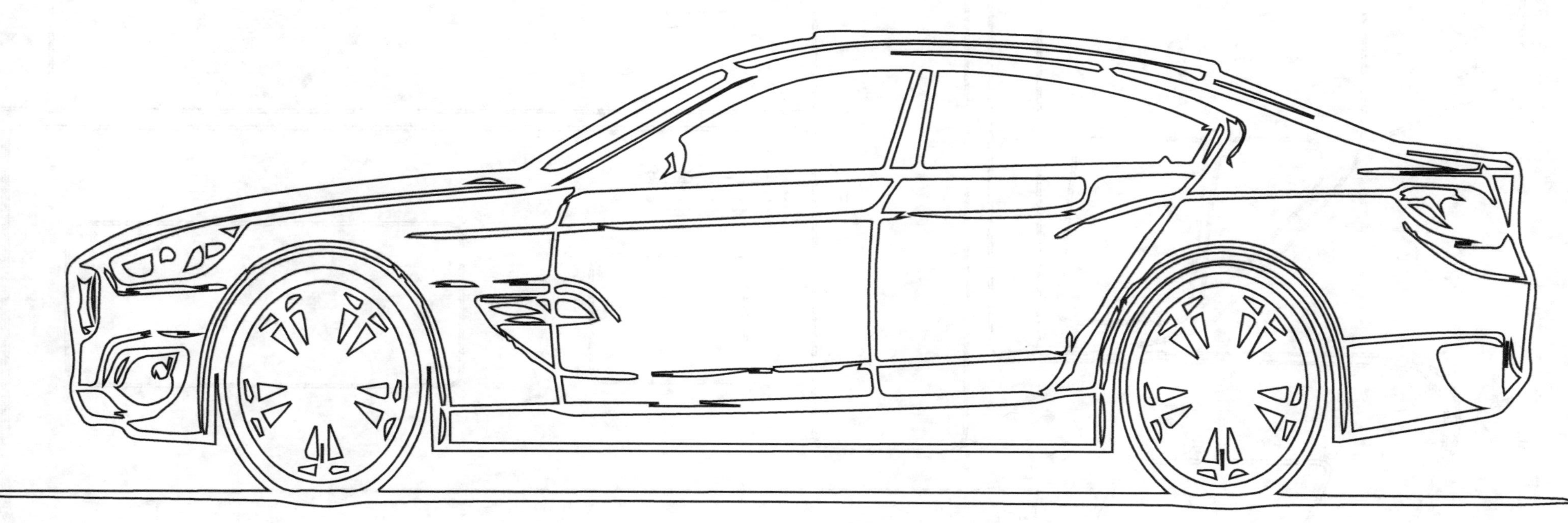

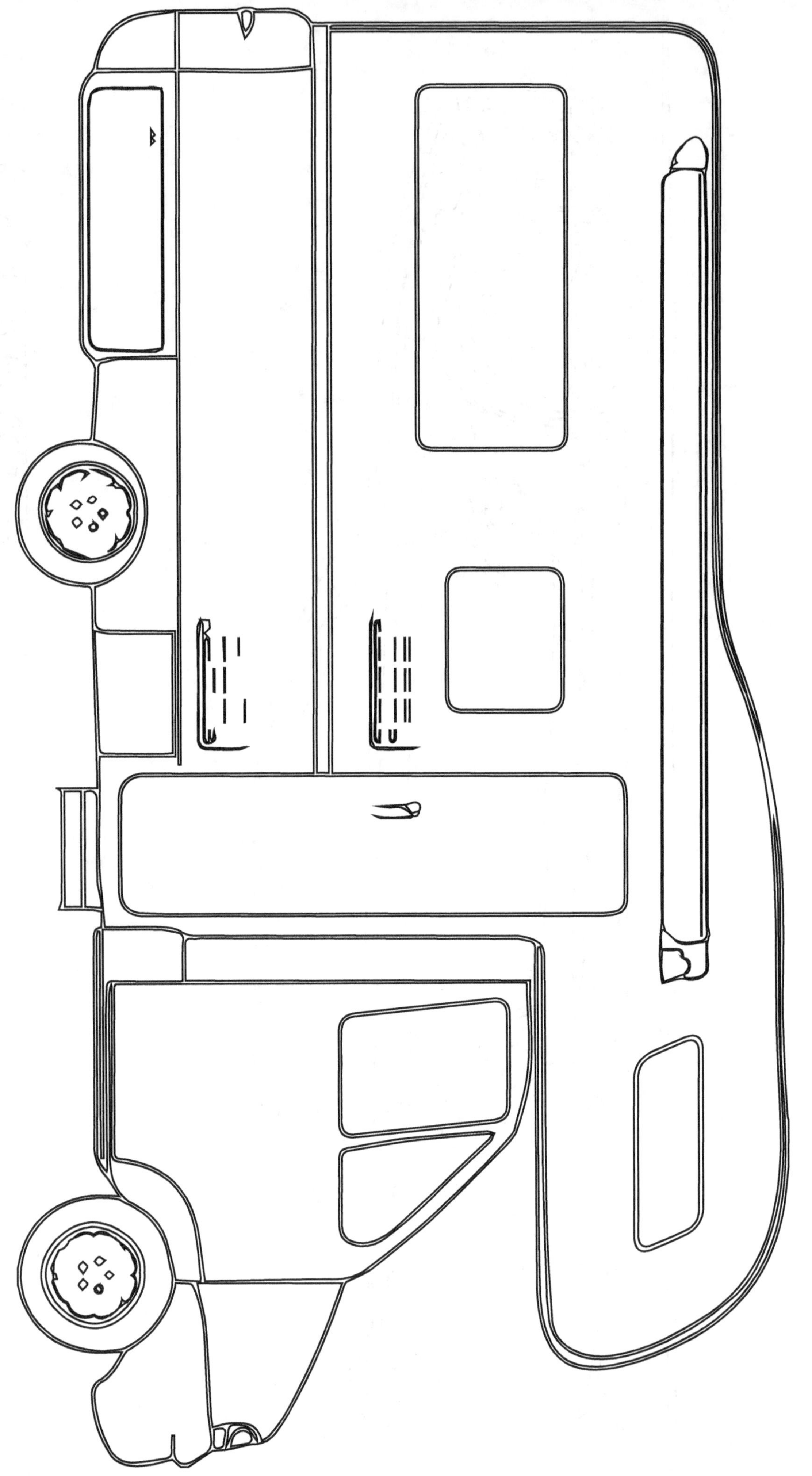
CAMPER VAN

POLICE CAR

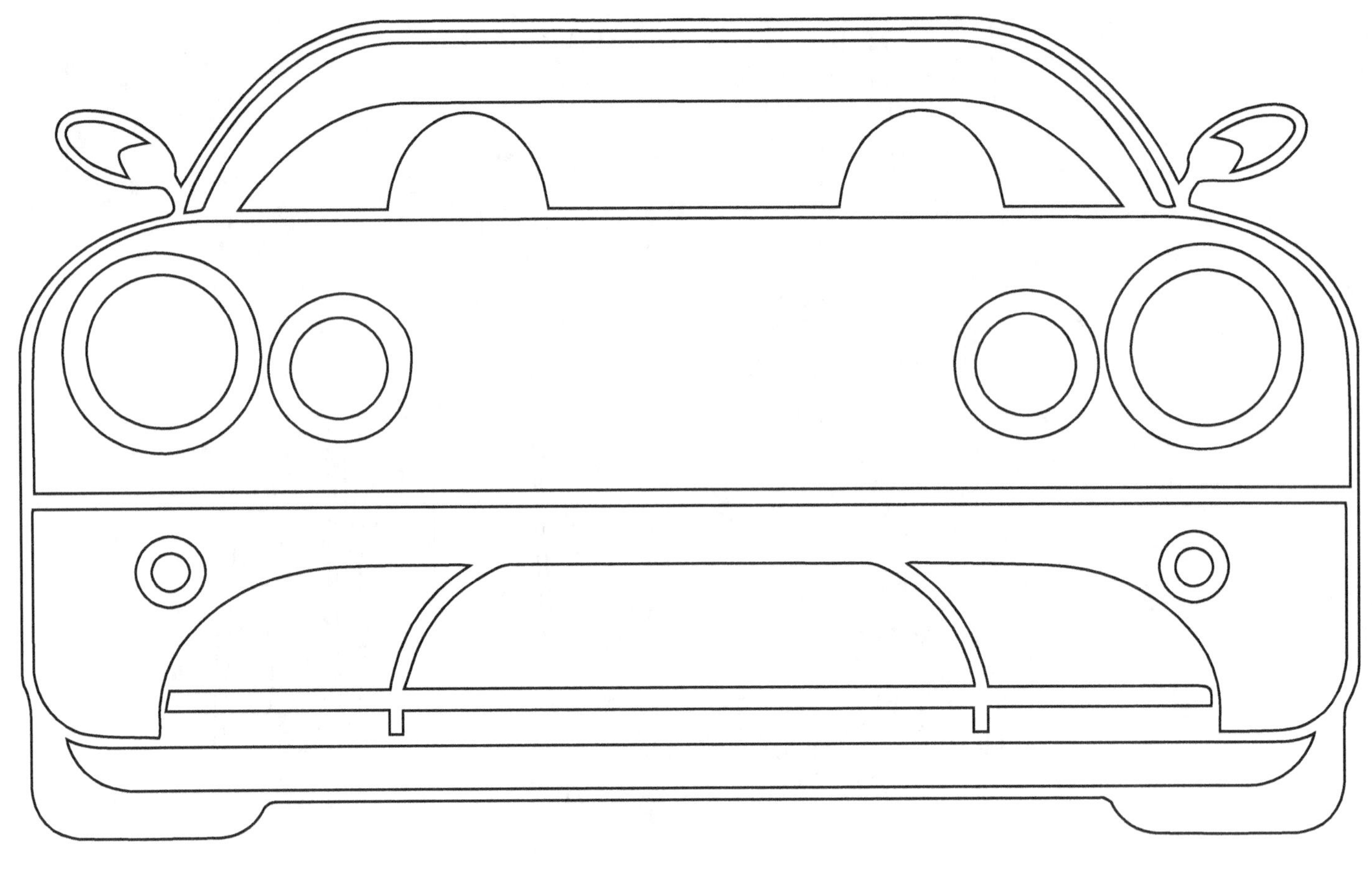

CONVERTIBLE

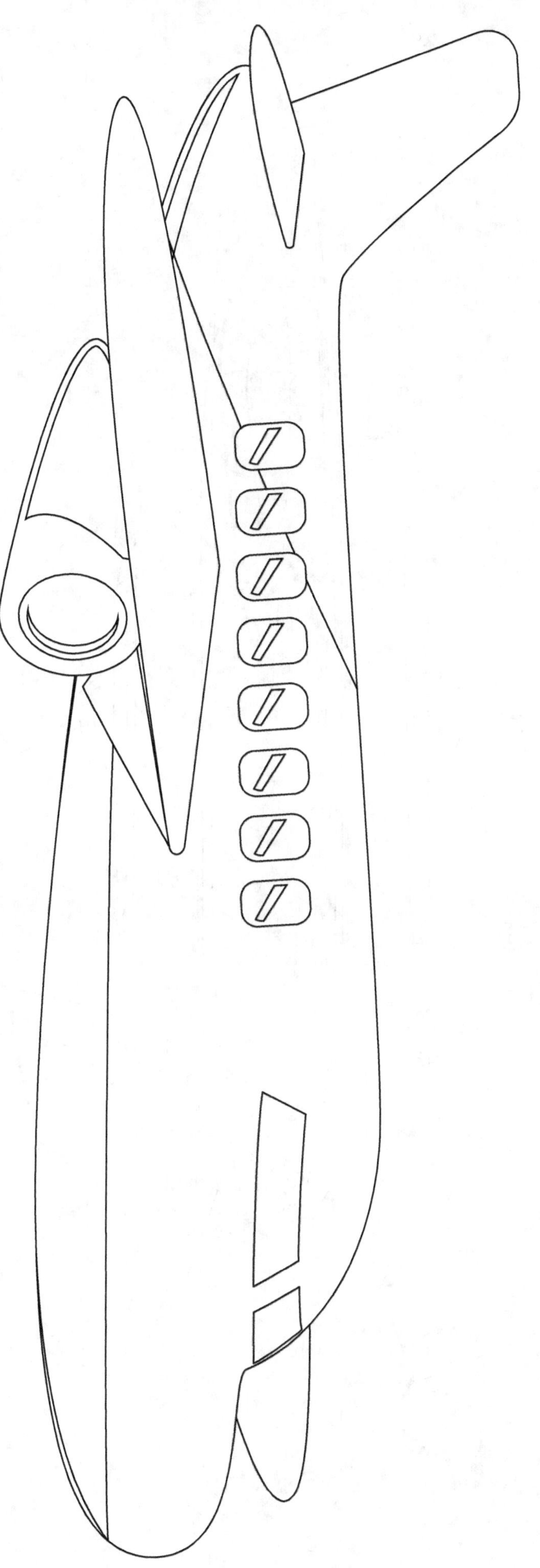

AIRPLANE

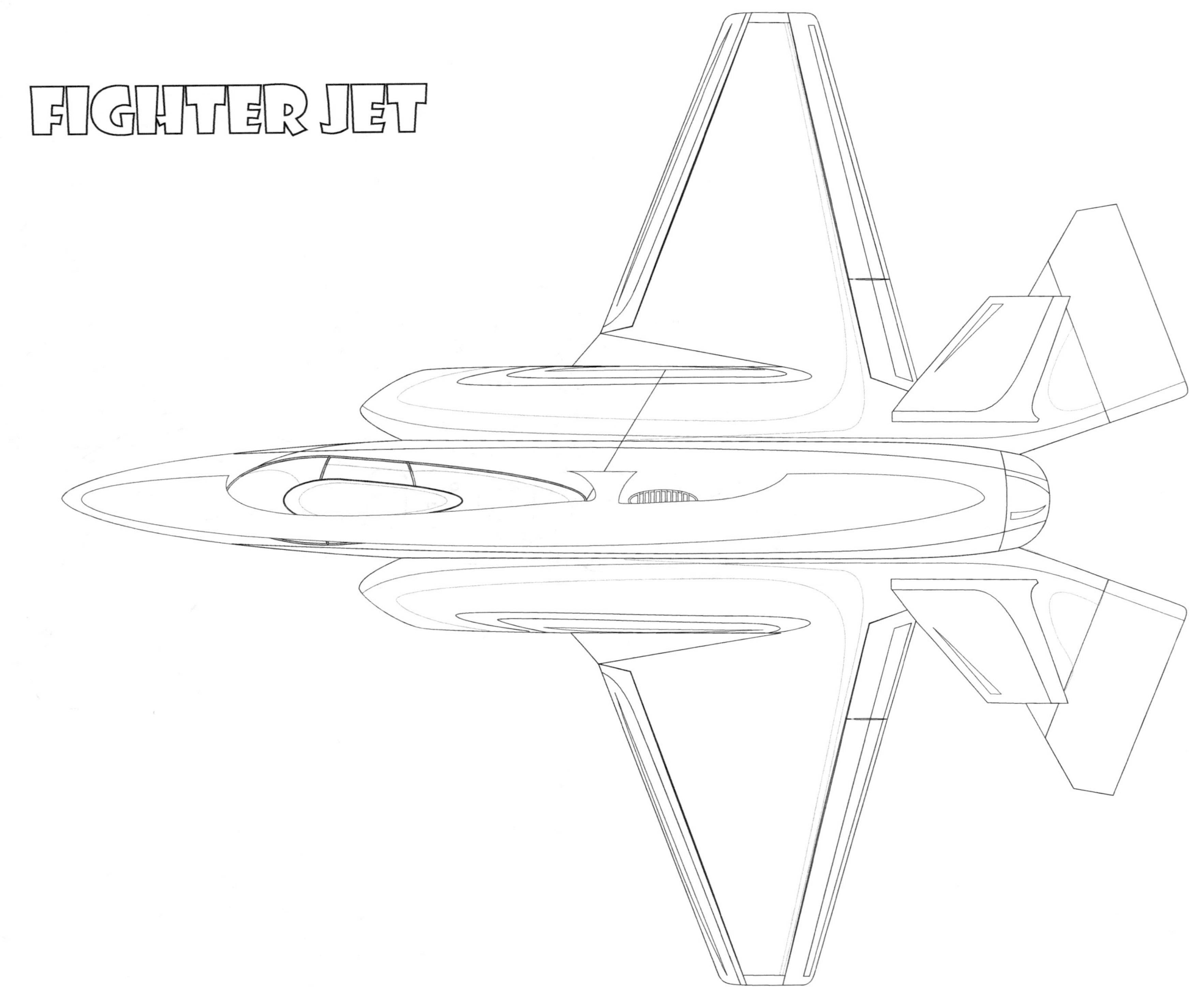

FIGHTER JET

PASSENGER AIRLINER

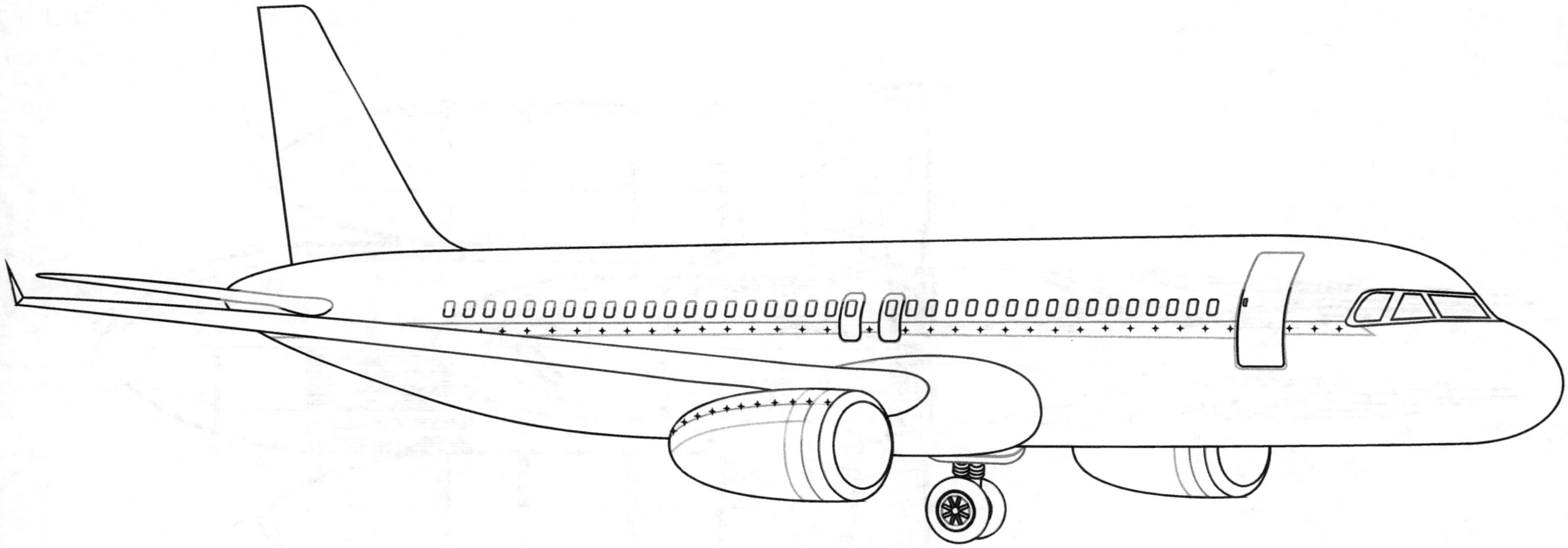

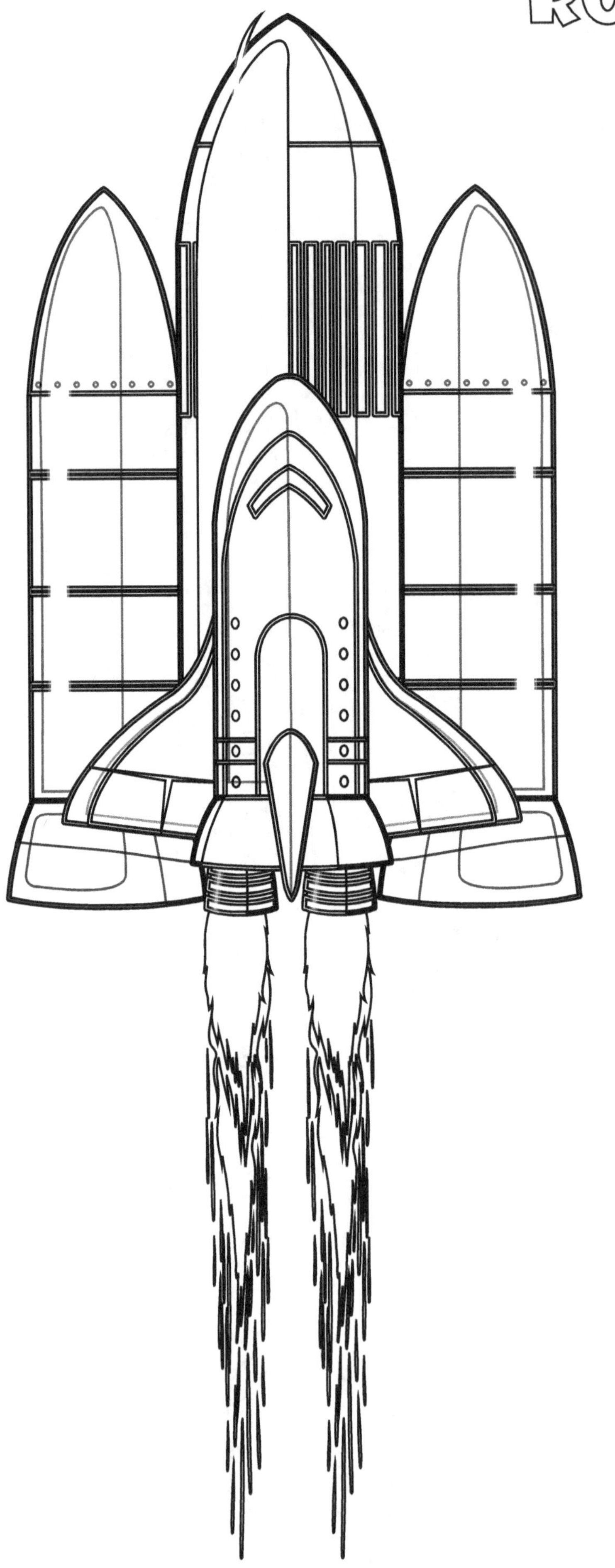

SPACE
ROCKET

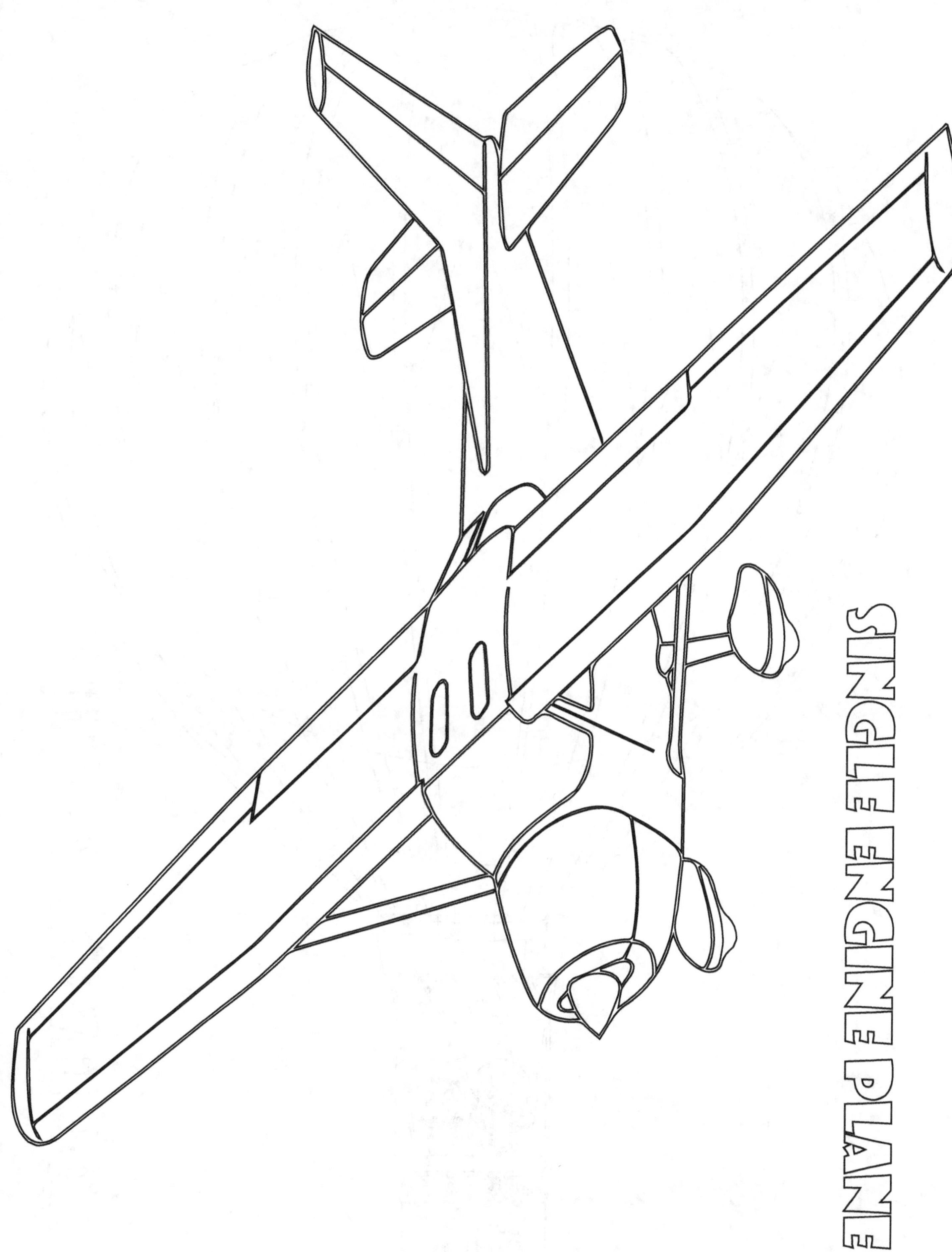
SINGLE ENGINE PLANE

HOT AIR BALLOON

MULTI-ENGINE AIRFACT

MONOPLANE

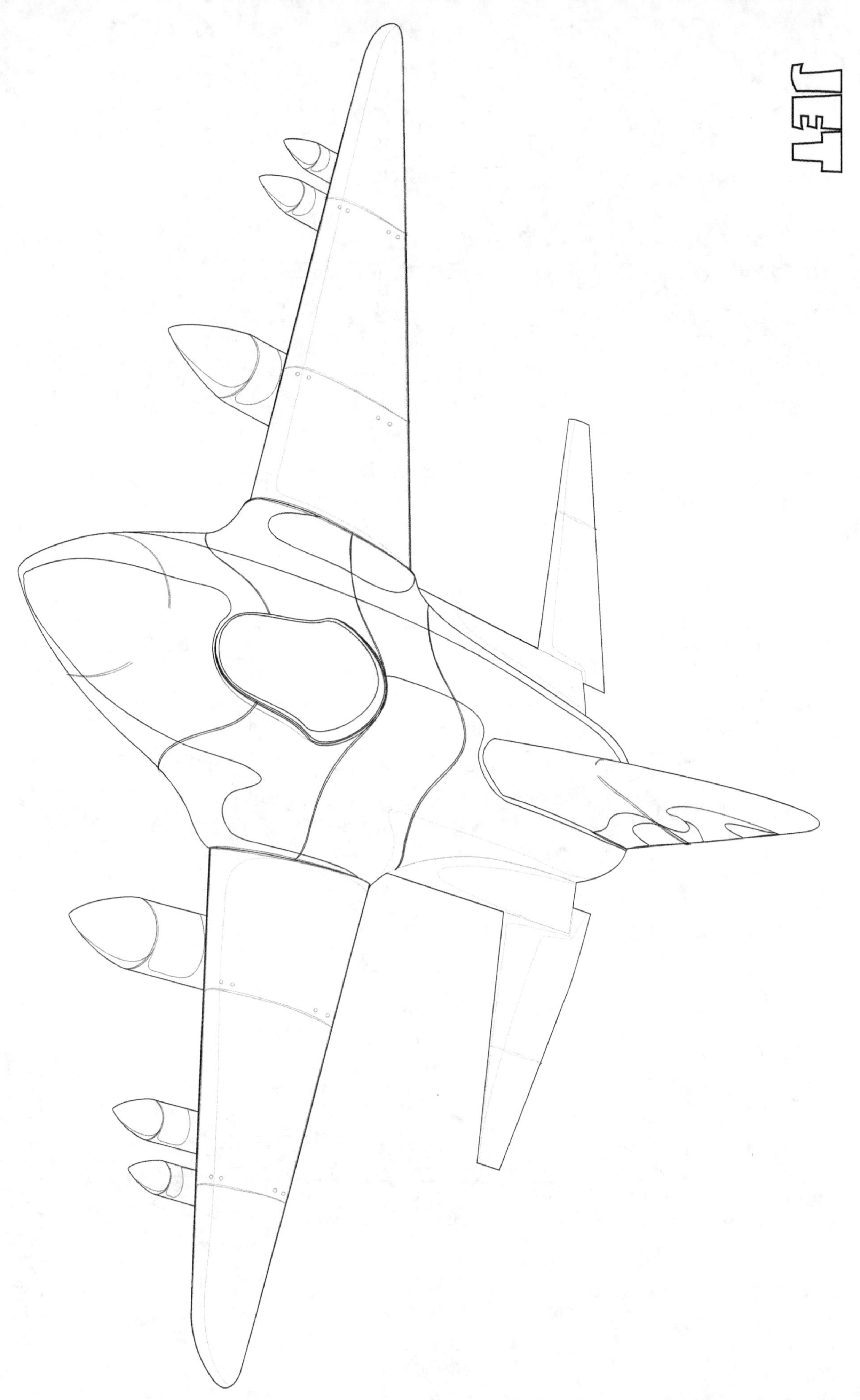

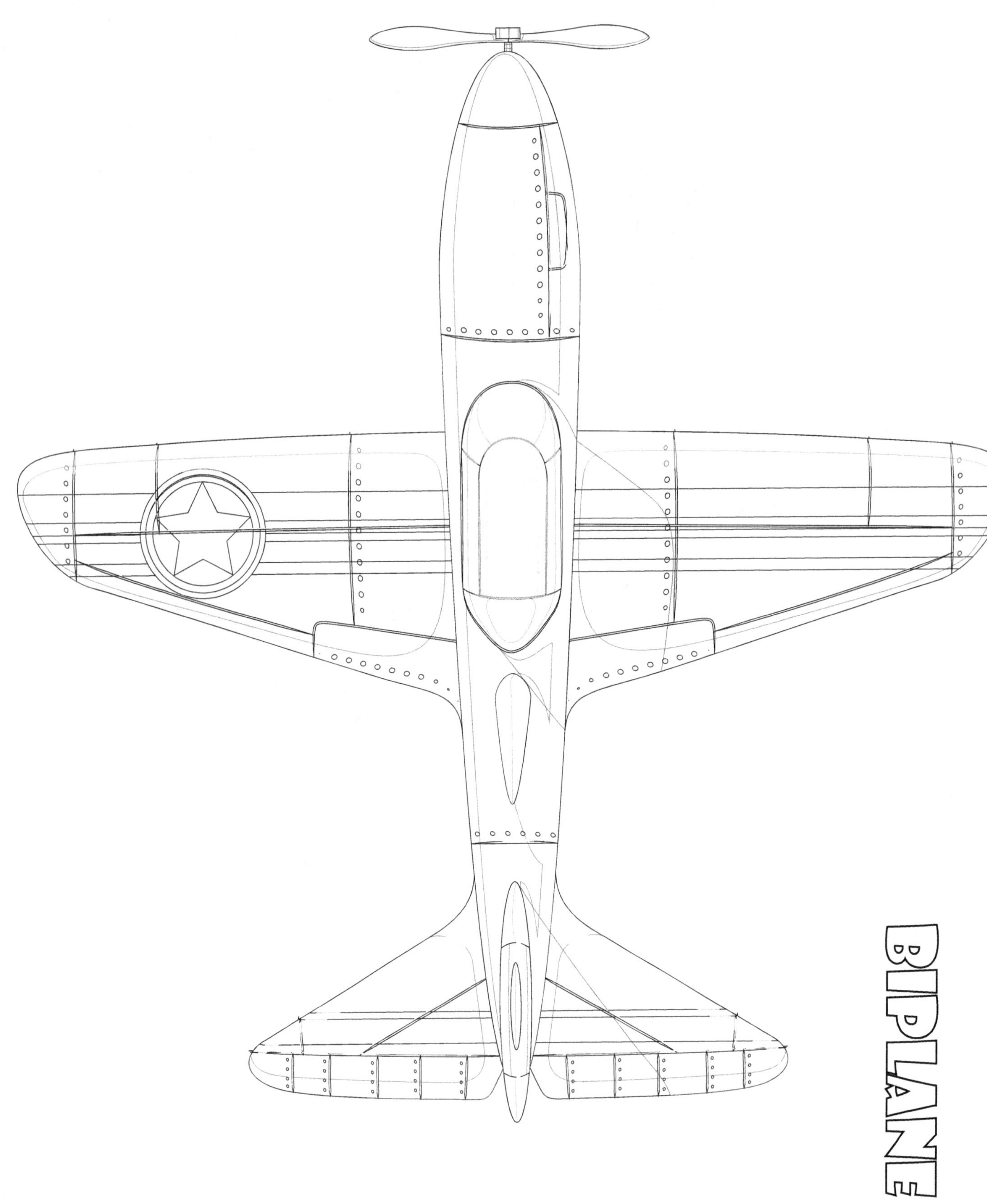
BIPLANE

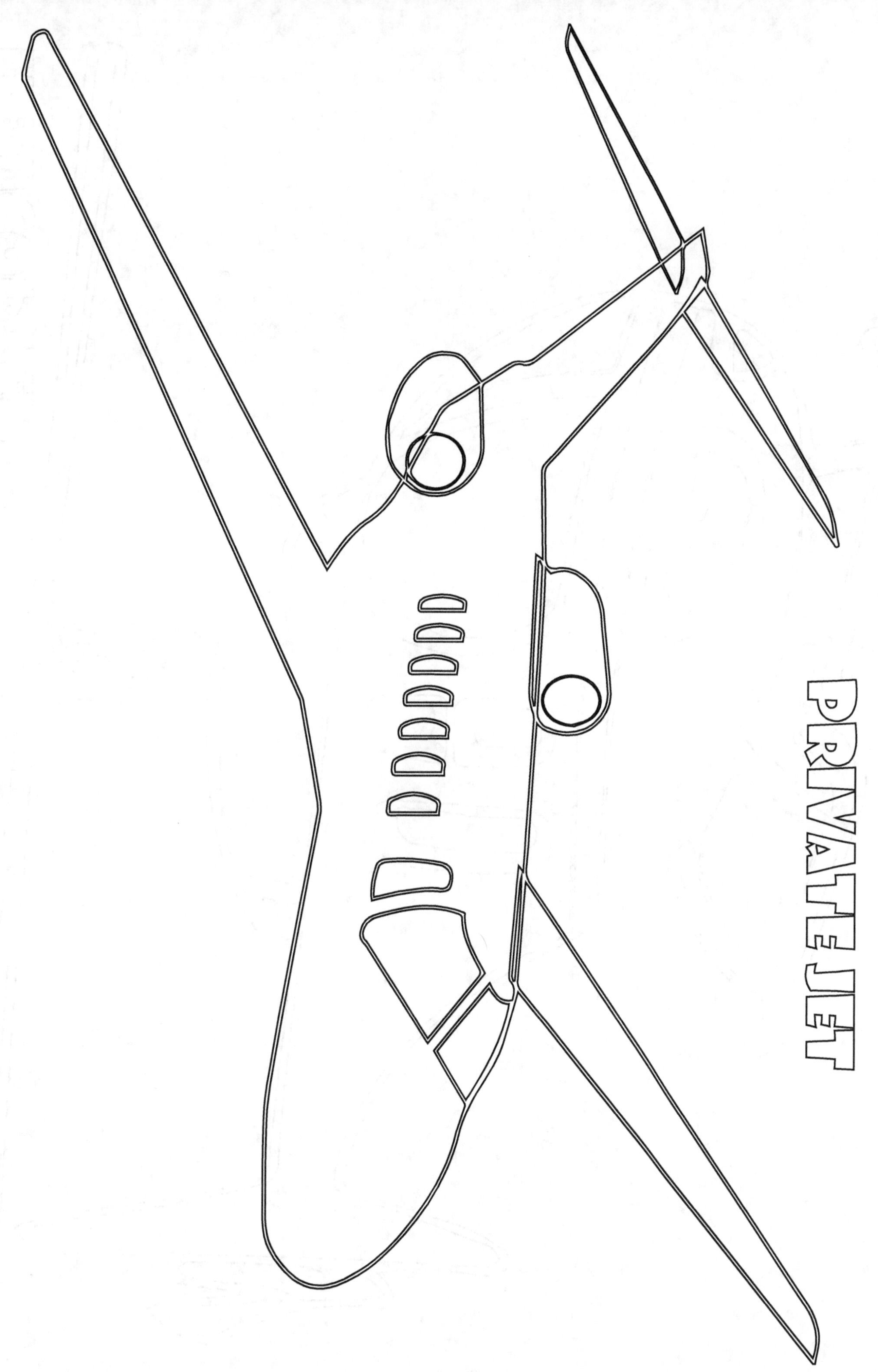

PRIVATE JET

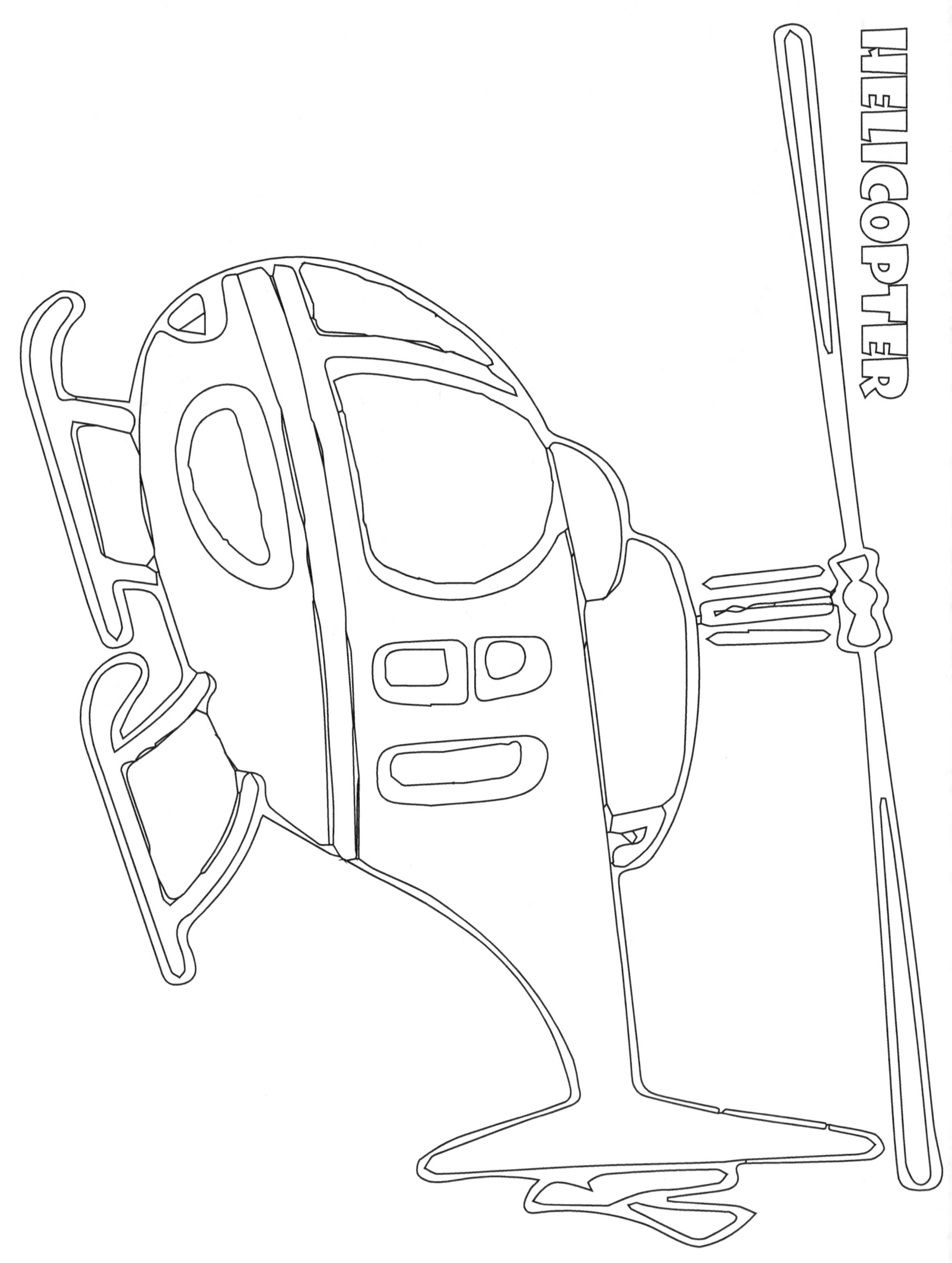

HELICOPTER

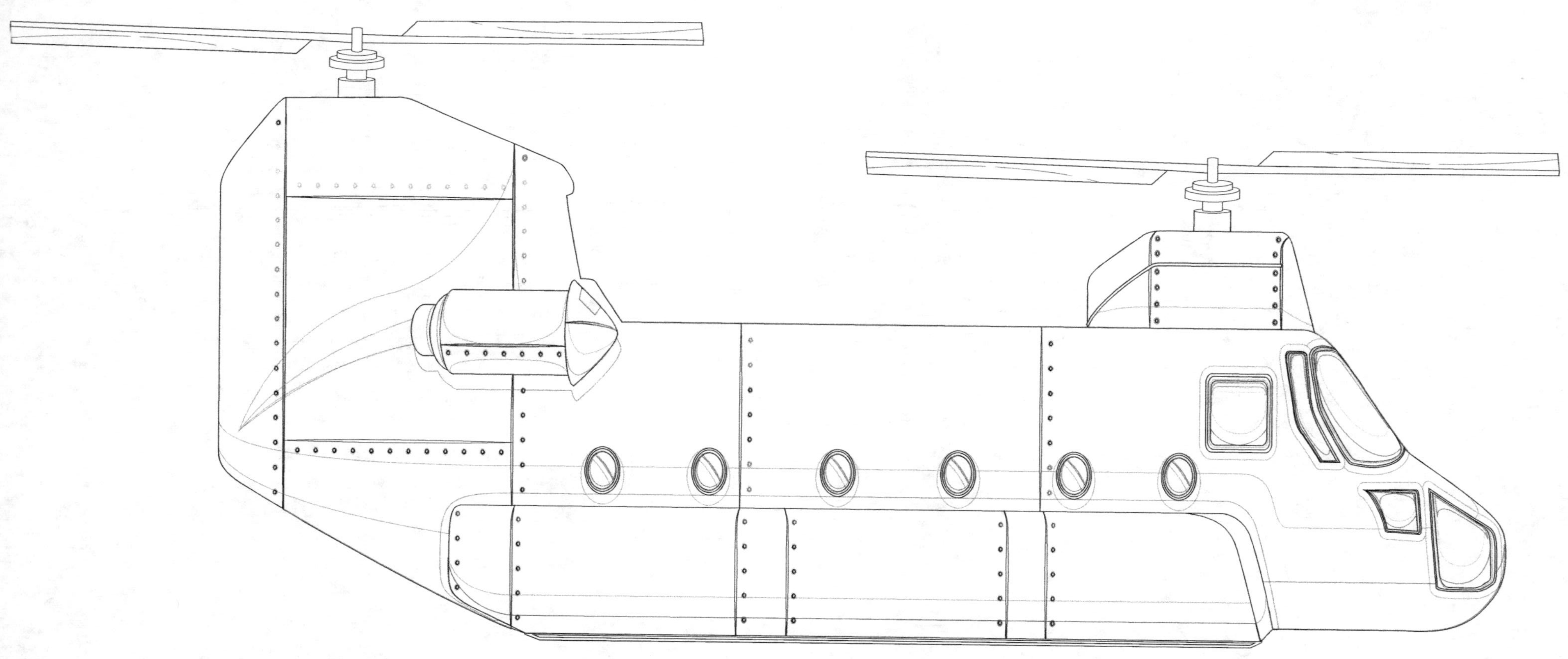

SHINOOK HELICOPTER

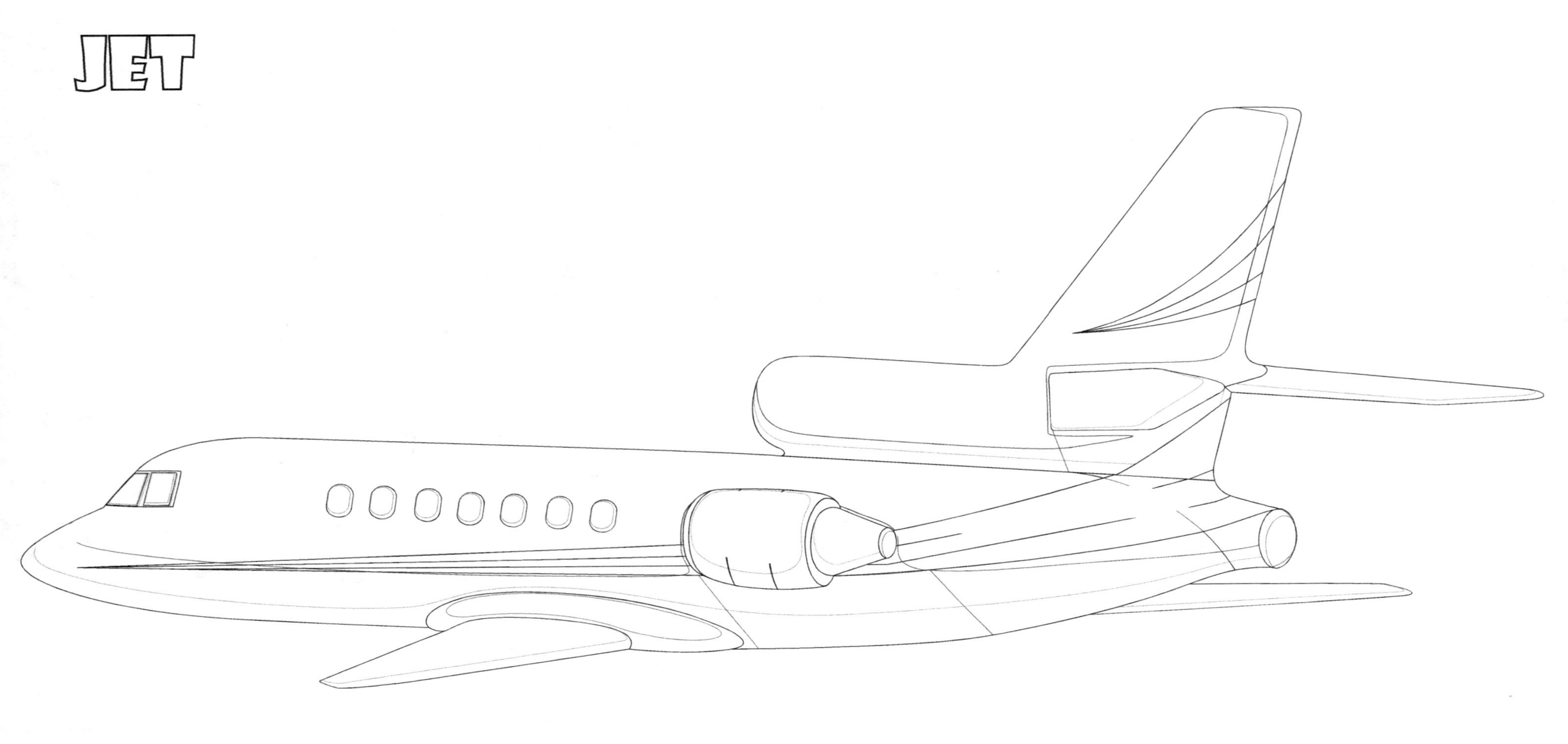
JET

www.ingramcontent.com/pod-product-compliance
Lightning Source LLC
Chambersburg PA
CBHW081431250726
48654CB00013B/1919